I0019246

**Temitope Takpor**

**Implementation and Evaluation of a Zigbee Network**

**Impressum / Imprint**
Bibliografische Information der Deutschen Nationalbibliothek: Die Deutsche Nationalbibliothek verzeichnet diese Publikation in der Deutschen Nationalbibliografie; detaillierte bibliografische Daten sind im Internet über http://dnb.d-nb.de abrufbar.
Alle in diesem Buch genannten Marken und Produktnamen unterliegen warenzeichen-, marken- oder patentrechtlichem Schutz bzw. sind Warenzeichen oder eingetragene Warenzeichen der jeweiligen Inhaber. Die Wiedergabe von Marken, Produktnamen, Gebrauchsnamen, Handelsnamen, Warenbezeichnungen u.s.w. in diesem Werk berechtigt auch ohne besondere Kennzeichnung nicht zu der Annahme, dass solche Namen im Sinne der Warenzeichen- und Markenschutzgesetzgebung als frei zu betrachten wären und daher von jedermann benutzt werden dürften.

Bibliographic information published by the Deutsche Nationalbibliothek: The Deutsche Nationalbibliothek lists this publication in the Deutsche Nationalbibliografie; detailed bibliographic data are available in the Internet at http://dnb.d-nb.de.
Any brand names and product names mentioned in this book are subject to trademark, brand or patent protection and are trademarks or registered trademarks of their respective holders. The use of brand names, product names, common names, trade names, product descriptions etc. even without a particular marking in this works is in no way to be construed to mean that such names may be regarded as unrestricted in respect of trademark and brand protection legislation and could thus be used by anyone.

Coverbild / Cover image: www.ingimage.com

Verlag / Publisher:
LAP LAMBERT Academic Publishing
ist ein Imprint der / is a trademark of
OmniScriptum GmbH & Co. KG
Heinrich-Böcking-Str. 6-8, 66121 Saarbrücken, Deutschland / Germany
Email: info@lap-publishing.com

Herstellung: siehe letzte Seite /
Printed at: see last page
ISBN: 978-3-8484-3609-5

Zugl. / Approved by: Durham, Durham University, 2009

## SCHOOL OF ENGINEERING

# IMPLEMENTATION AND EVALUATION OF A ZIGBEE NETWORK

### MSC RESEARCH PROJECT
BY
**TEMITOPE OLUWATOSIN MAKANJUOLA**

COURSE:
**MSC COMMUNICATIONS ENGINEERING**

SUBMISSION DATE:
**17TH AUGUST 2009**

TUTOR:
**MR PETER BAXENDALE**

i

# ACKNOWLEDGEMENTS

I acknowledge the grace of GOD upon my life. I give GOD all the glory for giving me wisdom and understanding. I would like to acknowledge Mr Peter Baxendale and Mr Tony that assisted and supported me during my research work. I am also grateful to my family and friends for their care and concern.

# SUMMARY

There is a growing need for compact devices that can interoperate with each other wirelessly and offer a wide range of applications. Wireless data transfer is normally being preferred to transmission of data via cables. In addition, consumers like using devices that save power because it leads to low cost. With the intention of meeting the consumer's needs, ZigBee Alliance developed a ZigBee wireless protocol which offers low power, low cost, reduced resource requirement and a standard set of specification. ZigBee permits inter-working capability between its devices from different products, since it is standard compliant.

ZigBee network performance was analyzed in this project, by carrying out experiments in an indoor environment. A comparison was done between ZigBee and a proprietary standard called MiWi wireless protocol, to reinforce ZigBee implementation.

RSSI and Average Delay performance indicators were used for the analysis done. Results showed that data loss was reduced in ZigBee than MiWi. In addition, the results obtained showed that ZigBee was designed for longer distance communication as compared to MiWi.

# PROJECT PLAN

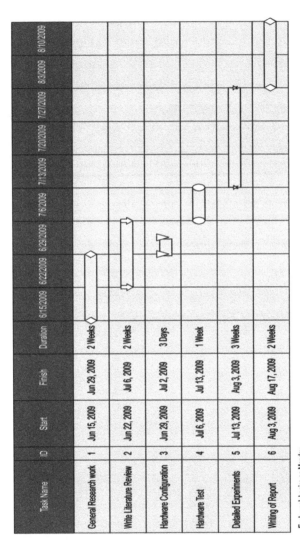

| Task Name | ID | Start | Finish | Duration | 6/15/2009 | 6/22/2009 | 6/29/2009 | 7/6/2009 | 7/13/2009 | 7/20/2009 | 7/27/2009 | 8/3/2009 | 8/10/2009 |
|---|---|---|---|---|---|---|---|---|---|---|---|---|---|
| General Research work | 1 | Jun 15, 2009 | Jun 29, 2009 | 2 Weeks | | | | | | | | | |
| Write Literature Review | 2 | Jun 22, 2009 | Jul 6, 2009 | 2 Weeks | | | | | | | | | |
| Hardware Configuration | 3 | Jun 29, 2009 | Jul 2, 2009 | 3 Days | | | | | | | | | |
| Hardware Test | 4 | Jul 6, 2009 | Jul 13, 2009 | 1 Week | | | | | | | | | |
| Detailed Experiments | 5 | Jul 13, 2009 | Aug 3, 2009 | 3 Weeks | | | | | | | | | |
| Writing of Report | 6 | Aug 3, 2009 | Aug 17, 2009 | 2 Weeks | | | | | | | | | |

Each week begins on Monday

# CONTENTS

# NOMENCLATURE

PHY – Physical Layer

MAC – Medium Access Control Layer

IEEE – Institute of Electrical and Electronics Engineers

NWK –Network Layer

APL – Application Layer

SSP – Security Service Provider Layer

HVAC – Heating Ventilating and Air Conditioning

SCADA – Supervisory Control and Data Acquisition

RF – Radio Frequency

ISM – Industrial Scientific and Medical

DSSS – Direct Sequence Spread Spectrum

TDMA – Time Division Multiple Access

CAP – Contention Access Period

GTS – Guaranteed Time Slot

CSMA-CA – Carrier Sense Multiple Access - Collision Avoidance

PAN ID – Personal Area Network Identifier

Demo Kit – Demonstration Kit

MCU – Microcontroller Unit

SPI – Serial Peripheral Interface

# CHAPTER 1

## INTRODUCTION

*"ZigBee is the global wireless language connecting different devices to work together and enhance everyday life [2]"*

ZigBee is a new standard from a corporation named ZigBee Alliance, which consists of more than 300 companies and was established in 2002 [2]. ZigBee is specifically designed for low data rate, low power and low cost applications.

The objectives of a ZigBee wireless network are to transmit data and save power as well, reduce cost, incorporate the standard into small chips, increase convenience and enhance reliability and security. ZigBee provides long battery life and, easy installation and maintenance methods. ZigBee network is usually referred to as self-healing and self-joining network [5].

ZigBee standard defines a protocol stack that is layered upon the PHY and MAC layers of IEEE 802.15.4 standard. The stack includes Network layer, Application layer and an optional Security Service Provider (SSP) layer.

ZigBee enables thousands of devices to communicate wirelessly per network and it is the only global standard for real time remote control and monitoring applications [3]. These applications include;

- Home Automation (switches, lighting control, security systems)
- Building Automation (environmental control, security)
- Industrial Automation (process measurement and control, compliance monitoring, system alarms)
- Health Care /Medical control and monitoring (patient and fitness monitoring, patients call points, emergency roll call)
- Environmental Monitoring (energy management, HVAC monitoring and control, temperature and humidity monitoring, SCADA)
- Telecommunication Services

1

- Consumer Products (TV, DVD, Universal Remotes)
- PC and gaming peripherals

In this project, ZigBee performance was assessed in two different indoor environments - engineering building and student residential area (Brackenbury - Ustinov College). A proprietary standard, MiWi wireless protocol was briefly analyzed for comparison with ZigBee protocol. Both protocol stacks were developed by Microchip Technology Incorporation.

# CHAPTER 2

## LITERATURE REVIEW

This chapter explains a general overview of ZigBee standard and a brief comparison between ZigBee and MiWi.

### 2.1 ZigBee Standard Overview

ZigBee is based on services offered by IEEE 802.15.4 standard, which was finalized in 2003 by IEEE [0]. The IEEE 802.15.4 standard defines a protocol for low-rate Wireless Personal Area Network (LR-WPAN) and its PHY layer works in three RF bands shown in Table 1.

Table 1: IEEE 802.15.4 RF Bands

| Frequency Band | Available Channels (Channel Number) | Maximum Data Rate |
|---|---|---|
| 2.4 GHz (ISM band) | 16 (11 - 26) | 250Kbps |
| 915MHz | 10 (1 - 10) | 40Kbps |
| 868 MHz | 1 (0) | 20Kbps |

A DSSS scheme is employed by the IEEE 802.15.4 standard and it is used in all the bands. The first band is available globally; the second and third bands are available in USA and Europe respectively. The total number of available channels is 27, but the MAC layer of the IEEE 802.15.4 standard can only use one of these channels at a time [0]. The MAC layer has a maximum packet length of 127 bytes [15] and its header is displayed in Table 2.

Table 2: MAC Header

| MAC Frame Control | Sequence Number | Destination PAN | Destination Address | Source Address |
|---|---|---|---|---|

3

### 2.1.1 ZigBee Network Devices and Topologies

ZigBee can be classified into three device types; coordinator, router and end device.

> Coordinator: is a Full Function Device (FFD) that is powered by a mains or battery source. The coordinator starts and manages the network. It enables other devices to join the network and allocates network addresses to them. There can only be a single coordinator per network.

> Router: is also an FFD. It allows more nodes to join the network, thereby increasing the physical range of the network. It relays received messages to devices, manages routing tables, and may perform monitoring and control functions. The router's source of power is from the mains or battery.

> End Device: can either be a Reduced Function Device (RFD) or an FFD, and it is powered by a battery source. It is the simplest device that performs monitoring and control functions, sends messages via the parent node (coordinator / router), and can not manage the network.

ZigBee wireless network supports three kinds of topologies and each must have a minimum of two ZigBee devices (a coordinator and an end device).

> Star Network: is referred to as a single hop network and it is shown in Figure 1. It comprises of one coordinator and one or more end devices which communicate directly to the coordinator, it does not support routers. An end device can only send messages to other end devices via the ZigBee coordinator, then the latter passes on those messages to the intended device.

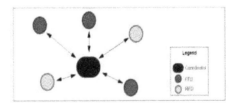

**Figure 1: Star Network Topology [4]**

➤ Cluster – Tree Network: consists of a coordinator, which acts as the root and transfers messages directly to the end devices or routers that serve as branches. The routers can in turn relay messages to other end devices connected to it that act as leaves of the tree network, and this enables the end devices not having to necessarily be within the radio range of the coordinator. This network is referred to as a multi hop network and it is shown below in Figure 2.

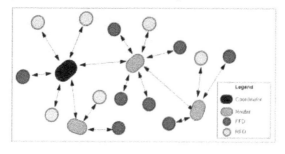

**Figure 2: Cluster Tree Topology [4]**

➤ Peer-to-peer / Mesh Network: is also called a multi hop network, therefore, similar to cluster – tree network. Although, the end devices (only FFDs) within radio range can communicate directly with each other and routers in range, as well. This means routing of messages does not necessarily have to be through the parent node, and thus reducing message latency and increasing network reliability. Refer to Figure 3 for a diagram of a mesh network.

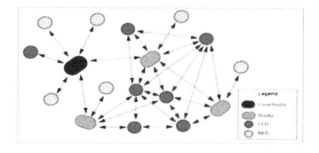

**Figure 3: Mesh Topology [4]**

5

## 2.1.2 Access Modes

The MAC protocol offers two types of access modes; beaconed and non-beaconed modes. In the beaconed mode, channel access and data transmission are based on a TDMA scheme. Therefore, predefined time slots are allocated to devices with the use of a superframe structure, which is shown in Figure 4.

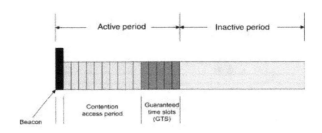

**Figure 4: Superframe Structure of IEEE 802.15.4 [1]**

A beacon request packet that precedes the superframe is periodically sent by the coordinator at the start of the network, and other devices join the network by synchronizing with the beacon. The superframe is divided into two major time slots; active and inactive periods. During the latter period, all devices go to sleep in order to save power and wake up before the end of the period to sense the next beacon. The active period includes the beacon packet, Contention Access Period (CAP) and Guaranteed Time Slot (GTS). The radio transceivers of the coordinator and router are always on throughout the active period, while the end devices are only active when transmitting and receiving packets in either CAP or GTS phase.

End devices need to compete to access the channel in the CAP, by using a slotted CSMA-CA protocol with a backoff algorithm, in order to avoid collision [4]. They can sleep when neither transmitting nor receiving in the CAP. The end devices are allowed to transmit and receive packets only in their assigned time slots, during the GTS phase.

The non-beaconed mode does not use the superframe structure like the beaconed mode, and as a result, time synchronization is absent. Devices transmit data when the channel is free and this is achieved by adopting an unslotted CSMA-CA protocol. The coordinator and router stay on throughout this mode, whereas, the end devices sleep while idle. The parent node of each end device needs to buffer messages that are directed to an end device that is in the sleep state. Afterwards, each end device will request its messages when it wakes up.

### 2.1.3  ZigBee Protocol Stack Architecture

The ZigBee Protocol stack shown in Figure 5, uses the PHY and MAC layers of the IEEE 802.15.4 standard as its two lowest layers respectively. These layers have been referred to in sections 2.1.1 and 2.1.2. The remaining upper layers are defined by the ZigBee standard and they are; the Network layer, Application Layer and SSP layer (optional).

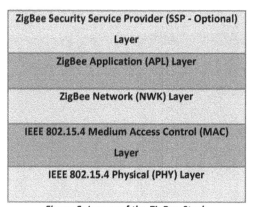

Figure 5: Layers of the ZigBee Stack

The network layer is responsible for ZigBee network formation and discovery, device address allocation and message routing. The latter enables messages to be relayed from the coordinators and routers, to the intended recipient.

The application layer defines ZigBee devices on the network and provides them with the capability of carrying out various applications. It also describes the messages transmitted between the devices. There are two types of application software profiles;

> ➤ Public profile: is created by the ZigBee Alliance. It permits devices to interoperate with each other and carry out specific task, irrespective of the manufacturer. An illustration of the interoperability operation is a switch device and a light bulb

7

device, which perform lightning task. There are few examples of public profiles that are presently available in the ZigBee market, they are; ZigBee Smart Energy and ZigBee Home Automation [2]. Other profiles are currently under development and they comprise building automation, personal health care and telecommunication services [2].

➢ Private profile: is created by a company or group of companies that operate ZigBee devices. Interoperability between devices is not necessary for this profile.

Lastly, the SSP layer offers security means and requires the application of the Advanced Encryption Standard [7].

### 2.1.4 Functions of a ZigBee Network

The functions of a ZigBee Network are described below, though they were briefly highlighted in the previous section 2.1.3.

➢ Network Formation: When a ZigBee coordinator is ready to form a ZigBee network, it searches its permitted channels in case of other existing coordinators. Therefore, the coordinator sets up its network based on channel energy level and networks discovered on its channels [4]. A unique 16 bit PAN ID must be chosen at start-up and it is used to identify the network.

➢ Network Addressing: Each ZigBee device has a globally unique 64 bit MAC address (IEEE Extended Unique Identifier) [6]. This address is also referred to as long address and it is used for communication when a device is about to join a ZigBee network. After successfully joining the network, it is assigned a 16 bit network address (short address) by its parent node. This new short address will then be used to communicate on the network. The short address is used rather than the long address because it reduces packet lengths and saves power.

➢ Joining the Network: Associated devices must send a correct association request packet to the coordinator so as to join the network. The coordinator then sends an acknowledgement packet which ensures that the sent packet was properly received. Afterwards, a data request would be sent by the devices and the coordinator would in turn send a corresponding association response packet. If an acknowledgement

8

flag was set during transmission, and the acknowledgement packet was not received before time out period, the transmitted packet would be retransmitted for a certain number of times before an error packet is issued (15). This feature makes a ZigBee network suitable for applications with quality of service (QOS).

➢ Network Association: Parent and child relationships are formed on a network to coordinate a wireless communication link between devices. This occurs when an old device on the network allows a new device to join it. Coordinators always act as parent nodes to routers and end devices. Routers can also act as parent nodes to end devices.

➢ Network transmission methods: Unicast, broadcast and multicast are different ways in which messages are transmitted on the network. The first type, allows messages to be directed to a specific device, while the second allows messages to be broadcasted to all devices on the network. Unicast and broadcast messages are sent via short addresses. Routers are capable of rebroadcasting messages to their child nodes. The MAC layer of a broadcast packet always shows a destination address 0xffff. The last type is similar to the second, but messages are sent to members of a specific group. The group members are assigned a group ID. Multicasting helps to reduce traffic on the network and group certain devices to carry out a specific application. A home automation example is grouping light switches and curtains in a living room together. When the lights are wirelessly switched off, the curtains will close automatically.

## 2.1.5 ZigBee Limitation

An alternate Personal Area Network coordinator capability is not supported in ZigBee protocol networks. It only permits one single ZigBee protocol. This would limit all the major work on the network to just the ZigBee Coordinator, therefore leading to a longer period of time for messages to be delivered. The effect of this would be seriously felt on a large network with much number of nodes.

## 2.2 ZigBee and Proprietary Standard (MiWi)

This sub-section briefly compares ZigBee with a proprietary standard – MiWi wireless protocol. MiWi is a simple proprietary standard that was designed by Microchip for low data rate, low cost, and short distance networks. This basic protocol can be used as an alternative to the compliant based ZigBee standard, and for applications that do not require interoperability with other ZigBee devices.

One of the reasons ZigBee is being preferred to MiWi is its support for larger network sizes and more hops between its devices. As a result, ZigBee is currently being used for wider range of applications. The size of the ZigBee network is more than 65,000 nodes, while MiWi has about 1,024 nodes. Packets can only travel a maximum number of 4 hops on MiWi network.

MiWi is also based on MAC and PHY layers of IEEE 802.15.4 standard and it supports ZigBee topologies. MiWi has three device types as well; PAN coordinator, coordinator and end device, which carry out same functions as ZigBee coordinator, ZigBee router and ZigBee end device respectively.

MiWi provides similar network features as ZigBee, but it does not support multicasting. For MiWi, messages can be broadcasted via long and short addresses alternatively or cluster socket link.

➢ Cluster socket link: is a dynamic communication link defined by MiWi, which exists between two devices (usually PAN coordinator and end device) on a network. This link can be established by pressing push button switches on each node within a certain period of time. It allows both devices know that they need to communicate with each other. The end device exchanges a cluster socket request packet for a cluster socket response packet from the PAN coordinator.

# CHAPTER 3

## EXPERIMENTS ON ZIGBEE AND MIWI NETWORKS

This chapter describes how ZigBee and MiWi networks were set up, and the various indoor experiments carried out. Same hardware platform was used for both networks. All ZigBee device types were configured for ZigBee network, while only PAN coordinator and end device were configured for MiWi Network.

### 3.1 Hardware Platform

The major required hardware for this project was a PICDEM Z demonstration kit. The kit was obtained from Microchip to evaluate ZigBee and MiWi networks. Included in the demo kit was; two PICDEM Z motherboards, two MRF24J40MA RF daughter cards, and ZENA wireless network analyzer. Figure 6 shows a cross section of the motherboard, RF card and ZENA network analyzer.

**Figure 6: Cross-Sectional View of Hardware Platform**

Each PICDEM Z board featured [8];

- PIC 18F4620 MCU (with a 64 KB of internal flash memory)
- RF daughter card connector (12-pin)
- Programmer RJ-11 connector (6-pin)

- RS-232 connector
- 9V DC to 3.3V DC regulator
- Temperature sensor
- LEDs (RA0 and RA1)
- Push button switches (MCLR/RESET, RB4 and RB5) to support applications.

The RF cards were IEEE 802.15.4 compliant 2.4 GHz transceiver modules, with integrated PCB antennas. It featured [9];

- 4-wire SPI (SCK, SDI, SDO and CS) interface to PIC 18LF4620
- Low current consumption (19 mA – TX mode, 23 mA – RX mode, and 2uA – Sleep mode)
- Operational voltage of 3.3V
- High RSSI dynamic range
- RF power of 0 dBm to about 36 dBm
- CSMA-CA mechanism
- Automatic ACK response
- Automatic packet retransmission
- Transmission range of around 100 metres outdoors and 20 meters indoors.

ZENA network analyzer was also IEEE 802.15.4 compliant and supported the 2.4 GHz spectrum. It functioned as a protocol stack configuration tool and a packet sniffer. It had a USB interface and was used to monitor and display; wireless network traffic, decoded packets and network topology, on a PC.

Another required hardware was Microchip's MPLAB ICD 3 in-circuit debugger / programmer with a USB and RJ-11 modular connectors. Lastly, there was an additional PICDEM Z board and RF transceiver module.

## 3.2 Hardware Configuration

The first step taken in the configuration of the hardware was to set up wireless nodes with the required boards, which were three PICDEM Z boards and three RF transceiver modules. The set-up was done by plugging each RF module into a 12-pin connector that was on every single PICDEM Z board. Therefore, the transceiver became internally connected to the PIC 18LF4620 MCU via the 4-wire SPI interface. The internal SPI connection and coordinator node are shown in Figure 7. See Appendix 1 for other nodes.

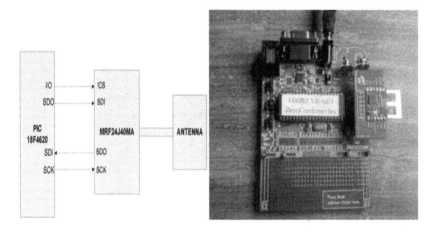

**Figure 7: Internal SPI Connection of a node and Coordinator node set-up**

Each node was then labeled coordinator, router and end device (RFD). A 9V wall adapter was used to power the coordinator, while 9V disposable batteries were used to power router and end device. The second configuration step involved is described in the next section 3.2.1.

### 3.2.1 Programming the Devices

The Programming environment for the nodes included; software package called MPLAB IDE version 8.33, MPLAB C18 compiler for the PIC 18F4620, and MPLAB ICD3 programmer. Complete demo application codes for ZigBee 2006 (version 2.0 -2.6) and MiWi protocol stacks were also included in the demo kit. The application codes developed by Microchip were written in C programming language. Two separate source files were provided for each device type, named, project file and .hex file (precompiled file). The flash memory of each PIC 18F4620 was programmed with an individual device code. The programming procedures that were carried out on each device are as follows;

- MPLAB IDE menu system was launched and displayed on the PC;
- PIC 18F4620 was selected from a family list of PIC 18 devices, that were on the menu;
- an appropriate .hex file was imported to the menu from the source directory;
- the ICD 3 programmer was connected to both PC (via a USB cable) and powered target device (through an RJ-11 cable);
- the LEDs on the programmer came on, which indicated that the ICD 3 was active;
- 'program' was selected on the menu to program the device;
- Lastly, the programmer was disconnected from both device and PC respectively.

Refer to Figure 8, for the programming set-up and an indication that the devices were successfully programmed.

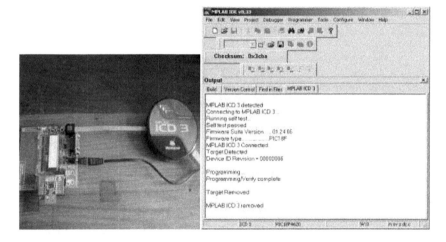

**Figure 8: Programming Set-up and indication of a successful programmed Device**

Later on, the demo was modified to carry out specific experiments which are explained in section 3.4. And each time the demo was modified; few lines of code in the original project file was changed, compiled (by the MPLAB C18) and saved as a .hex file. Then the devices were programmed appropriately by following the procedures above.

## 3.3 Running Application on Programmed Devices

The loaded demo on the devices was initially run for both ZigBee and MiWi. Although, it was modified before the experiments were performed. While the application ran, ZENA and the hyper terminal console were launched on the PC to view the network traffic and information within the demo, respectively. Necessary settings on the ZENA menu system were; device type, power source and network traffic channel, which were all set appropriately.

### 3.3.1 Running ZigBee Application

Demo application for ZigBee demonstrated how messages were transmitted on a ZigBee network by the multicast method. Messages were directed to group 4 members only and each member of the group was requested to send back a number of bytes of data to the requester. The application was run between the coordinator and the end device, and later ran with the inclusion of the router.

In the first application ran, the network was formed by a powered coordinator and this was indicated by the coming on of the coordinator's LEDs (RA0 and RA1). The end device was then enabled to join the network after it had being powered. Figure 9 shows the ZENA display of beacon request packet from the coordinator, association request packet from the end device and association response packet.

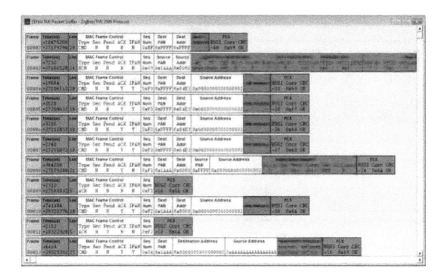

**Figure 9: ZENA display of request and response packets between Coordinator and End Device**

Afterwards, the end device was added to group 4 by pressing its RB4 button and its RA0 was turned on which indicated it was a member group 4. The coordinator was able to send messages to the end device after its RB5 button was pressed. RB4 and RB5 buttons were programmed to add / remove devices from group 4 and to send messages to group 4, respectively. Whenever the group messages were sent, the RA1 of the end device toggled on and off. This visually indicated that it had received the messages and responded to them.

In the second application ran, router joined the network after the network had being formed by the coordinator. The end device later joined and was associated with the router (parent node). Figure 10 shows the ZENA display of beacon request packets, association request packets from the devices and association response packets. The short address (0x1430) of the end device was different from that of the first application ran, which was 0x796F. This was so because it was assigned by the router, and not the coordinator. The End device was added to group 4 and the router relayed the group messages from the coordinator to it. The requested number of bytes was routed to the coordinator through the router. The steps involved in the relay of messages are further explained in section 3.4.2.

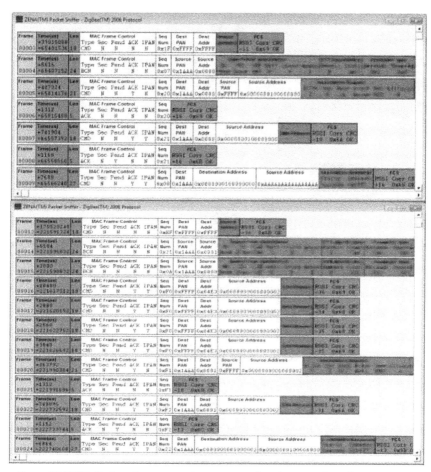

**Figure 10: ZENA display of request and response packets between Coordinator, Router and End Device**

### 3.3.2 Running MiWi Application

MiWi demo application demonstrated the transmission of messages on a MiWi network by the broadcast method (through the use of a cluster socket link). After the PAN coordinator and end device were already on the network, a cluster socket link was established between them. This was done when their RB5 buttons were pressed within a second at the same time. During the establishment, a cluster socket request (report ID 0x10) and cluster socket response (report ID 0x11) were exchanged and displayed on the ZENA, see Figure 11. RB4 on the end device was pressed to send messages to the PAN coordinator, while RA1 LED on the PAN coordinator toggled to indicate it had received the messages.

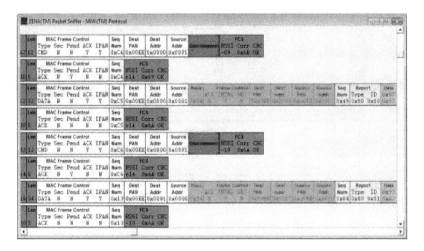

**Figure 11: ZENA display of request and response packets between MiWi Coordinator and End Device**

## 3.4 Experimental Methods

Experiments were carried out within the engineering building and student residential area (Brackenbury), after the programmed devices (with modified demo applications) were up and running. During the experiments, specific parameters were used to analyze the performance of ZigBee and MiWi Networks, and correct device types were used on each network. All desired measurements were read off from the ZENA display. The experimental tests are described in sections 3.4.1 and 3.4.2, and they were repeated 3 to 5 times.

### 3.4.1 Line of Sight Test (LOS - within Engineering Building)

This test involved direct transmissions between a coordinator and an end device. The devices were placed in visual contact at approximately equal heights above the ground. Measurements were taken along a corridor at 12 intervals with an incremental distance of $n\lambda$. Where, $\lambda$ is the wavelength in metres and n is a multiple number (10 was chosen for this test). Equation 1 shows a relationship between λ, c (speed of light with a constant value of $(3 * 10^8)$ ms$^{-1}$), and f (frequency of the transceiver).

$$c = \lambda * f \qquad\qquad \text{Equation 1}$$
$$\lambda = (3 * 10^8) \text{ ms}^{-1}/ \text{ 2.4 GHz}$$
$$\lambda = 0.125 \text{ m}$$

Therefore,

$$n\lambda = 10 * 0.125 = 1.25\text{m}$$

The coordinator was stationed at the end of the corridor while the end device was separated from it at distances ranging from 1.25 meters to 15 meters. Group messages were sent from the coordinator to the end device and the latter responded with the requested number of bytes. See Figure 12 for the ZENA display of ZigBee and MiWi network topologies, and Appendix 3 for the packets transmitted. The network topologies showed the long addresses of the nodes while short addresses of the nodes were displayed on the transmitted packets. The aqua node is the coordinator and the yellow node is the end device.

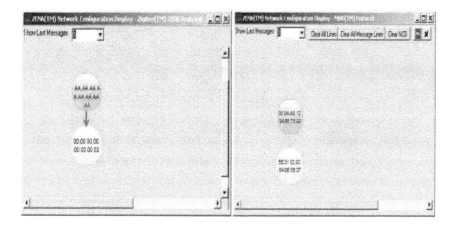

Figure 12: ZENA display of ZigBee and MiWi Network Topologies

19

The parameter used during this test was the Received Signal Strength Indication (RSSI), which is a measured value of the power present in a received packet. The test was performed to evaluate the effect transmit power ($P_t$) and distance separation (between nodes) had on RSSI value. LOS test specifically done for ZigBee network was called Test A and the LOS test done to compare ZigBee and MiWi was termed Test B. RSSI is a measurement of the power present in transceiver

- LOS Test A: RSSI readings were taken for three values of transmitted power (0 dBm, -10 dBm and -30 dBm), as the distance separation was increased. The transceiver's default transmit power was 0 dBm, so the codes were modified to enable the transceivers transmit in the desired power.
- LOS Test B: RSSI values (as a function of distance) were taken for a constant maximum transmit power 0 dBm.

LOS Tests A and B results are shown in section 4.1.

### 3.4.2 Tests within Brackenbury

The tests involved; direct transmissions between a coordinator and an end device (not in visual contact with each other), and transmissions with a router included, which relayed messages between the end device and the coordinator. Both transmissions were carried out for ZigBee network and were called Test C. Direct transmission was done for MiWi and compared with that of ZigBee, this was called Test D

Average Time was the parameter used for the evaluation of both networks. It was the period of time taken for the coordinator to send packets to the end device and receive packets from the end device correctly. The Average Time was measured as a function of packet length. Test readings were taken for 5 to 8 various packet lengths and the maximum was 80 bytes, since it was stated from section 2.1 that The MAC layer has a maximum packet length of 127 bytes.

Two major groups of tests were performed and Average Time readings were taken through walls, within a single flat and across floors.

<u>Transmissions within a single flat</u>: Tests C and D were carried out by placing devices in two scenarios; Living room (coordinator) – Room 5 (end device), and Living room (coordinator) – corridor (router) – Room 5 (end device). Figures 13 and 14 show an illustration of how packets were sent on the ZigBee network, in each scenario.

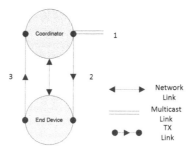

**Figure 13: Transmission Routes on a ZigBee Network**

In figure 13, the coordinator sent a multicast packet and waited for an internal signal (not transmitted wirelessly to be captured by the ZENA) from the end device. The internal signal indicated that the end device was a member of the group. Then the coordinator sent the message to the end device and the latter responded by sending a packet. There were three steps involved in the transmission process.

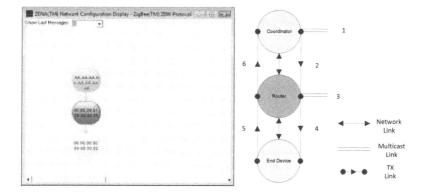

**Figure 14: Transmission Routes on a ZigBee Network through Router**

In figure 14, the coordinator sent a multicast message and waited for an internal signal from the router. Since the router was not a member of the group, it rebroadcasted the packet and waited for an internal signal from its child node (end device). Then the end device responded to its parent node by sending the requested packet, and the router relayed the packet to the requester (coordinator). There were six steps involved in the transmission process.

Transmissions across floors: Tests were carried out across four floors (from ground floor to first, second and third floors) and did not include transmission with a router. These tests were termed Test E, and Average Time readings were recorded for both ZigBee & MiWi Networks, at a constant packet length of 40 bytes.

Results for Tests C, D are shown in section 4.2.and Test E is shown in section 4.3

# CHAPTER 4

## RESULTS AND DISCUSSION

### 4.0 Results and Discussion

The results obtained during the experiments were analyzed and discussed in this chapter.

### 4.1 RSSI Results

See Appendix 2 Table of Results for Test A and Test B.

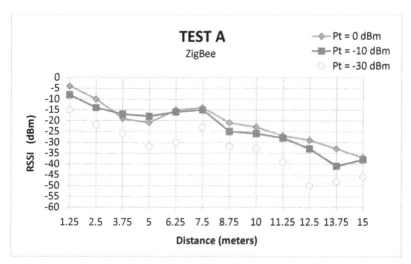

**Figure 15: RSSI as a function of distance between nodes for three values of Transmit Power**

Test A results show that there was a decrease in RSSI as distance was increased. There were fluctuations due to obstruction from people walking across the corridor and reflections from chairs placed along the corridor. Change in transmit power reduced the RSSI values especially at -30 dBm. RSSI values for 0 dBm and -10 dBm were slightly different, and this shows that a great reduction in transmit power would make a major difference in the received signal. 0 dBm gave the highest values, therefore, an increase in transmit power led to a better ZigBee Network performance.

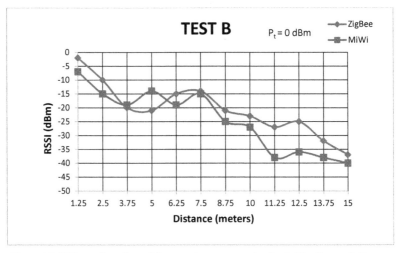

**Figure 16: RSSI as a function of distance between nodes for 0 dBm Transmit Power**

Test B results show that RSSI values obtained for both Networks were slightly different for the first half of separation distances - 1.25 meters to 7.5 meters. Later on the RSSI values for MiWi dropped from separation distance 8.75 m to 15 meters. This showed that MiWi was designed for shorter distance applications in an indoor environment. Tests were not carried out in an outdoor environment, so a general conclusion could not be made for MiWi being strictly designed for short distance networks.

## 4.2 Average Time Results

See Appendix 2 Test C and Test D for table of results.

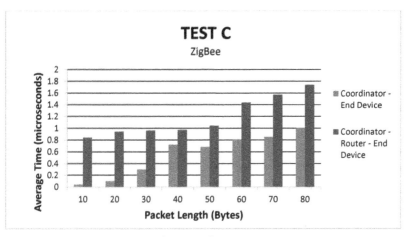

**Figure 17: Average Time as a function of Packet Length on a ZigBee Network**

Figure 17 indicates that it took a longer time for packets to be relayed through the router. Theoretically, router plays a vital role of extending the physical range of the network but this would probably be done at the cost of time. Since the results clearly show that average time is greatly increased with the inclusion of a router on ZigBee Network. From Figure 14, six steps were taken to transmit packets between the coordinator and the receiver, and the effect of this was shown in the result.

The Average Time for the relay transmission is nearly more than double of that of a direct transmission. Furthermore, increase in packet length linearly reduces with the Average Time.

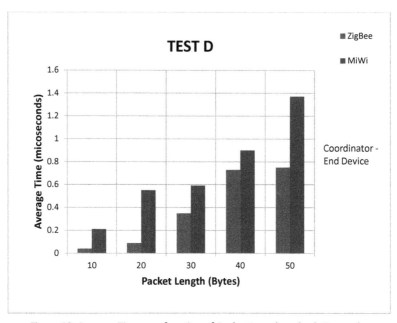

**Figure 18: Average Time as a function of Packet Length on both Networks**

Test D shows a linear increase in Average Time for both ZigBee and MiWi. And it also shows that it takes longer time for packets to be transmitted on a MiWi network when compared to a ZigBee network. It is perceived that if a MiWi coordinator (that functions as a router) was used to relay messages between the coordinator and end device, the delay would be far greater than that obtained in Test C. But that kind of experiment could not be carried out due to time limit.

## 4.3 RSSI and Average Time Results

Test E results are displayed in Table 3 along with corresponding RSSI values (transmit power was set to 0 dBm).

**Table 3: TEST E Results**

| Across Floors | Average Time (microseconds) Coordinator - End Device | | RSSI (dBm) Coordinator - End Device | |
|---|---|---|---|---|
| | ZigBee | MiWi | ZigBee | MiWi |
| Ground Floor - 1st Floor | 1.69 | 1.85 | -43 | -49 |
| Ground Floor - 2nd Floor | 1.98 | No response from the End Device | -49 | No received packet |
| Ground Floor - 3rd Floor | No response from the End Device | No response from the End Device | No received packet | No received packet |

The average time delay increased enormously across floors. There was no response from the end device for transmission across ground floor and third floor for a ZigBee Network. These results are due to the fact that people introduced reflection and fading effects.

Very high RSSI values were gotten for transmit power of 0dBm and this was due to the transmission path being obstructed by thick walls and doors. Packets were lost due to increase in floors.

# CHAPTER 5

## Conclusion

This research work has been able to analyze the performance of a ZigBee network and also compared ZigBee with a proprietary standard, MiWi. ZigBee was designed for longer distance communication as compared to MiWi, and this was shown in the results obtained by the use of 2 performance indicators (RSSI and Average Time). Results showed that data loss was reduced in ZigBee than MiWi.

Throughout the 5 weeks of experiment, the battery power was never low, although it is not long enough to conclude that power was saved. But ZigBee standard adopts a good access mechanism to save power.

Since time limited the possible number of readings that can be obtained, future work can be done on the analysis of both Networks. An important further analysis would be; obtaining data throughput to see if almost 250 Kbps can be obtained, because theory states that 250 Kbps is the maximum data rate for 2.4 GHz frequency band.

# REFERENCES

[1]  Holger, K. and Willig, A. (2007)  Protocols and Architecture for Wireless Sensor Networks.   $5^{th}$ ed.   West Sussex England: John Wiley & Sons.

[2]   Heile, B. (2006) ZigBee Overview. [online]  Available from: http://www.zigbee.org/LearnMore/Tutorials/tabid/278/Default.aspx [accessed $18^{th}$ June 2009]

[3]  ZigBee IDC Brochure: Wireless Mesh Networking Products and Solutions. [online] Available from:   http://www.zig-bee.co.uk/ [accessed $3^{rd}$ August 2009]

[4]  Derrick P. L. (2006)  Microchip ZigBee-2006 Residential Stack Protocol Application Note. Microchip Technology Inc. U.S.A.

[5]  Beckley, K. () What is ZigBee? [online]  Available from: http://www.zig-bee.co.uk/Zigbee/tabid/869/Default.aspx [accessed $3^{rd}$ August 2009]

[6]   Armholt, M. (2006)  Implementation of the ZigBee Network Layer and Evaluation of Route Discovery Initiation.  Masters thesis. Lulea University of Technology.

[7]  Garcia, R.R. (2006)  Understanding the ZigBee Stack. Freescale Semiconductor Inc. [online]  Available from: http://www.eetasia.com/ART_8800402260_499488_TA_ecf61bd2.HTM [accessed $15^{th}$ June 2009]

[8]  Microchip Technology Inc. (2008)  PICDEM Z Demonstration Kit User's Guide. U.S.A. [online] Available from: http://www.microchip.com/stellent/idcplg?IdcService=SS_GET_PAGE&nodeId=1406&d DocName=en021925&part=DM163027-2 [accessed $29^{th}$ June 2009]

[9]  Microchip Technology Inc.  (2008)  MRF24J40MA Data Sheet 2.4 GHz IEEE Std. 802.15.4 RF Transceiver Module. U.S.A. [online]  Available from: http://www.microchip.com/stellent/idcplg?IdcService=SS_GET_PAGE&nodeId=2664&p aram=en535767 [accessed $6^{th}$ July 2009]

# APPENDICES

## Appendix 1: Device Types

**Appendix Figure 19: Router**

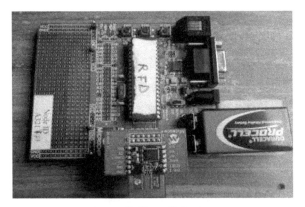

**Appendix Figure 2: Router**

# Appendix 2: Table of results

### Appendix Table 1: TEST A

| nλ | Distance (meters) | RSSI Values (dBm) measured for three Pt values | | |
|---|---|---|---|---|
| | | $P_t = 0$ dBm | $P_t = -10$ dBm | $P_t = -30$ dBm |
| 1λ | 1.25 | -4 | -8 | -15 |
| 2λ | 2.5 | -10 | -14 | -22 |
| 3λ | 3.75 | -19 | -17 | -26 |
| 4λ | 5 | -21 | -18 | -32 |
| 5λ | 6.25 | -15 | -16 | -30 |
| 6λ | 7.5 | -14 | -15 | -23 |
| 7λ | 8.75 | -21 | -25 | -32 |
| 8 λ | 10 | -23 | -26 | -33 |
| 9λ | 11.25 | -27 | -28 | -39 |
| 10λ | 12.5 | -29 | -33 | -50 |
| 11 λ | 13.75 | -33 | -41 | -48 |
| 15 | 15 | -37 | -38 | -46 |

**Appendix Table 2: TEST B**

| nλ | Distance (meters) | RSSI Values (dBm) measured for Pt = 0 dBm | |
|----|----|----|----|
| | | ZigBee | MiWi |
| 1λ | 1.25 | -2 | -7 |
| 2λ | 2.5 | -10 | -15 |
| 3λ | 3.75 | -20 | -19 |
| 4λ | 5 | -21 | -14 |
| 5λ | 6.25 | -15 | -19 |
| 6λ | 7.5 | -14 | -15 |
| 7λ | 8.75 | -21 | -25 |
| 8 λ | 10 | -23 | -27 |
| 9λ | 11.25 | -27 | -38 |
| 10λ | 12.5 | -25 | -36 |
| 11 λ | 13.75 | -32 | -38 |
| 15 | 15 | -37 | -40 |

**Appendix Table 3: TEST C**

| Packet Length (Bytes) | Average Delay (microseconds) ZigBee Network | |
|---|---|---|
| | Coordinator - End Device | Coordinator - Router - End Device |
| 10 | 0.04 | 0.84 |
| 20 | 0.1 | 0.94 |
| 30 | 0.3 | 0.96 |
| 40 | 0.72 | 0.97 |
| 50 | 0.68 | 1.04 |
| 60 | 0.81 | 1.44 |
| 70 | 0.85 | 1.57 |
| 80 | 1 | 1.74 |

**Appendix Table 4: TEST D**

| Packet Length (Bytes) | Average Delay (microseconds) Coordinator - End Device | |
|---|---|---|
| | ZigBee | MiWi |
| 10 | 0.04 | 0.21 |
| 20 | 0.09 | 0.55 |
| 30 | 0.35 | 0.59 |
| 40 | 0.73 | 0.9 |
| 50 | 0.75 | 1.37 |

## Appendix 3: ZENA Network Analyzer Results

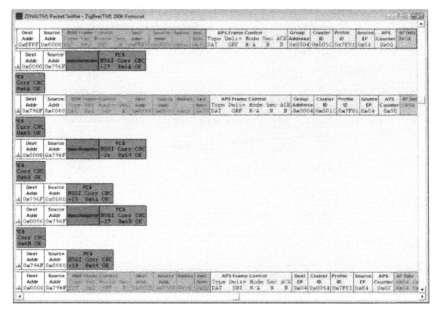

**Appendix Figure 3: Transmitted packets between ZigBee Coordinator and ZigBee End Device**

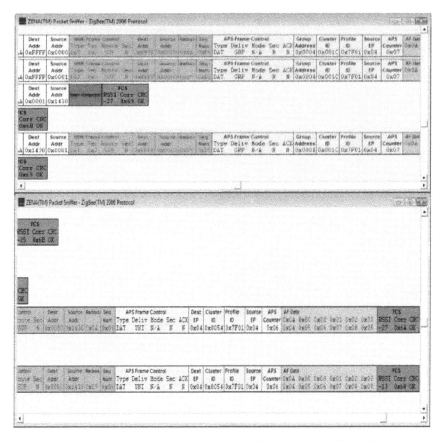

**Appendix Figure 4 Transmitted packets between ZigBee Coordinator, ZigBee Router and ZigBee End Device**

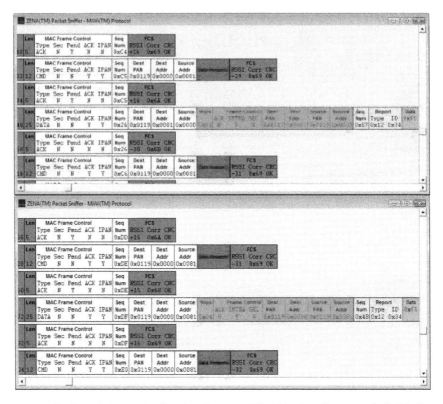

**Appendix Figure 5: Transmitted packets between MiWi PAN Coordinator and MiWi End Device**

www.ingramcontent.com/pod-product-compliance
Lightning Source LLC
LaVergne TN
LVHW042352060326
832902LV00006B/545